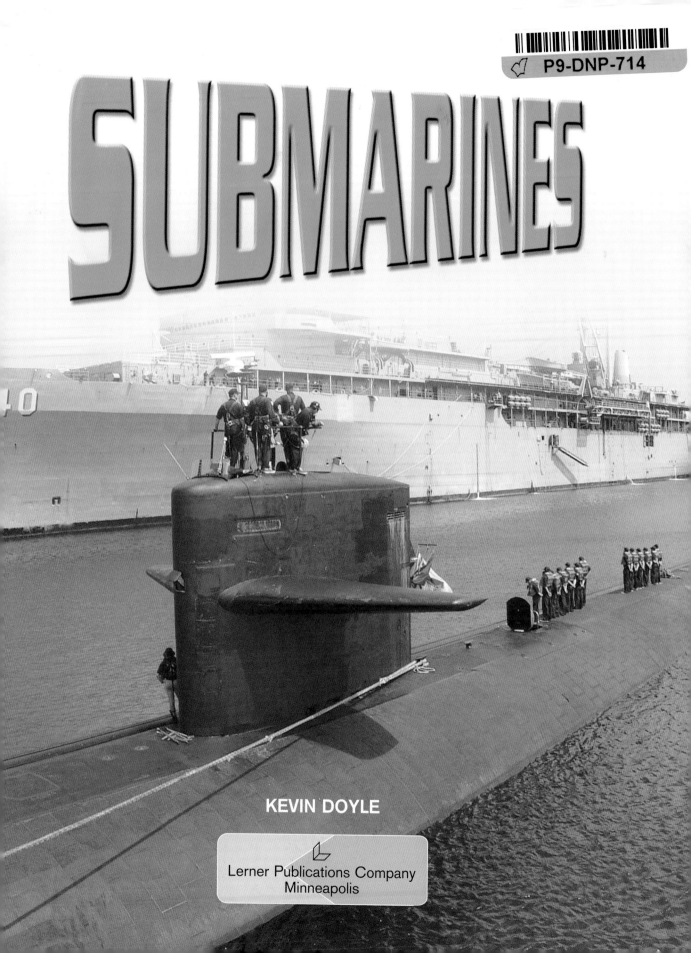

SUBMARINES

KEVIN DOYLE

Lerner Publications Company
Minneapolis

First American edition published by Lerner Publications Company.

Copyright © 2003 by The Brown Reference Group plc.

Lerner Publications Company.
A division of Lerner Publishing Group
241 First Avenue North
Minneapolis, MN55401 U.S.A.

Website address: www.lernerbooks.com

Library of Congress Cataloging-in-Publication Data

Doyle, Kevin.
 Submarines / by Kevin Doyle.
        p. cm. -- (Military hardware in action)
Includes index.
Summary: Profiles some of the different submarines used by the
United States Navy and other navies around the world, describing their
designs, weapons, and uses.
  ISBN 0–8225–4704–X (lib. bdg.)
1. Submarines (Ships)--United States--Juvenile literature. 2.
Submarines (Ships)--Juvenile literature. [1. Submarines (Ships).] I.
Title. II. Series.
  V858.3 .D69 2003
  359.9'383--dc21   2002013598

Printed in China
Bound in the United States of America
1 2 3 4 5 6 – OS – 08 07 06 05 04 03

This book uses black and yellow chevrons as a decorative element on some headers. They do not point to other elements on the page.

Contents

Introduction

Among the shifting gray-blue shadows of the ocean lurks a nuclear-powered submarine. Silently, a hatch opens and a **cruise missile** bursts out of the water. It sweeps clear of the surface. Then it changes course for its distant target. A nuclear submarine is the ultimate weapon in any nation's collection of weapons.

MISSILE GONE

A Poseidon **ballistic missile** bursts upward from beneath the waves.

  >> **cruise missile** – a guided missile that flies at low level to its target

Early Start

Submarines are among the most powerful weapons in a modern navy. But their origins go back over two centuries. As long ago as the American Revolution (1775–1783), inventors were working on ways to attack surface ships from below the waterline.

TURTLE TACKLES EAGLE

In 1776 the American submarine pioneer David Bushnell tried to sink the British warship HMS *Eagle*. He managed to steer beneath the ship in an egg-shaped wooden craft named the *Turtle*. Bushnell was not able to drill through the British warship's hull. It had been reinforced with steel plate.This illustration shows the cranks that turned the *Turtle's* corkscrew propellers and its hand-operated rudder. It also details the drill for boring holes through wooden hulls.

USS HOLLAND

The U.S. Navy's first submarine, the USS *Holland*, was commissioned in 1900. It had a crew of six and three torpedoes. The long, tube-shaped hull had a rear engine, front torpedo tubes, and a central crew area. This basic design was adopted for all future submarines.

>> **ballistic missile** – a long-range guided missile that free falls onto its target

World Wars

During the two world wars of the 1900s, submarines became important weapons in **strategic** warfare. They threatened both surface warships and supply routes. Submarines were able to affect the outcome of the conflicts.

World War I

During World War I (1914–1918), U-boats (German submarines) came close to crippling the British war effort. They sank supply ships traveling from North America.

U-BOAT TERROR

A German U-boat in the rough seas of the North Atlantic. After sighting an enemy, the U-boat dived. It then attacked unseen.

>> **strategic** – relating to political or long-term military goals

World War II

During World War II (1939–1945), submarines went after ships sailing between North America and Europe. U.S. Navy and Allied submarines attacked Japanese shipping in the Pacific. Their efforts helped force the Japanese to surrender in 1945.

ATLANTIC STRANGLEHOLD

A view from the tower of a surfaced U-boat. German U-boats sank more than 20 percent of Allied supply ships between 1940 and 1943. Their success almost brought the isolated British Isles to collapse. After Allied **codebreakers** began to figure out German navy signals, the U-boats became the targets instead.

PACIFIC PERIL

A U.S. Navy submarine on its way to the Pacific in 1943. As a small island nation, Japan needed imports from overseas to fight the war. The U.S. Navy defeated the Japanese navy at Midway and Leyte Gulf. After that, Japanese supply ships were at the mercy of Allied submarines.

>> **codebreaker** = a person who deciphers messages in secret code

The Submarine's Role

Submarines have both **tactical** and strategic roles. As tactical weapons, they stalk and sink enemy warships and supply ships, called tenders. A strategic submarine carries long-range missiles. These can threaten a nation or an entire continent.

HUNTER-KILLERS

The U.S. Navy fast attack submarine USS *Salt Lake City* next to a submarine supply tender. Also called "hunter-killers," fast attack submarines are tactical weapons. They are equipped with torpedoes and missiles that are designed to sink enemy ships.

Nuclear Deterrent

Ballistic missile submarines are a deterrent force. They deter, or discourage, an enemy from attacking, because of the damage they can do.

CRUISE MISSILES

Some submarines have cruise missiles. Cruise missiles are long-range weapons designed to strike targets on land. They can be fitted with nuclear **warheads**. Nonnuclear cruise missiles are tactical. They are used for destroying individual military targets. Nuclear cruise missiles are strategic weapons of mass destruction that threaten whole populations.

BALLISTIC MISSILE SUBS

A ballistic missile nuclear submarine plows through the Pacific, with its missile hatches open. These submarines can launch long-range missiles from any ocean to almost anywhere on land or sea. Nuclear-powered submarines can stay underwater almost indefinitely. They are almost impossible to find or track.

The Submarine's Role

In addition to attack and ballistic missile submarines, there are other **submersibles** that do different jobs. Some gather intelligence, and some are designed for **sabotage**. Others act as rescue and recovery craft.

The U.S. Navy research submarine USS *Dolphin*. Research submarines do not attack other ships. They stay out of sight to test systems and equipment that may be used in combat subs. They also observe and report on enemy positions and coastal defenses.

These U.S. Navy Special Forces are preparing to board an inflatable boat during operations in the Middle East in 2002. Some submarines are adapted for special operations. They may be used to secretly carry soldiers to a combat area.

>> **submersible** – any boat that can function underwater

HELPING OUT

A deep-sea rescue submersible sits on the deck of a Los Angeles class attack submarine. Submarines are divided into classes—categories in which ships of a similar type are grouped. Submarines have become much safer than they were in the 1950s and 1960s, when the first nuclear-powered and nuclear-armed submarines appeared. However, a submarine that is in trouble needs special equipment to lift it or to free the trapped crew.

PART OF THE PACK

Submarines can operate freely and almost at will. But they are still part of a larger force. They sometimes help to protect a fleet at sea. Sometimes subs operate in small groups for greater protection and firepower.

Submariners

Because of the dangers involved with undersea combat, submariners have always been regarded as a special group. Like fighter pilots, submariners attract public attention. Some have become legends.

German Aces

German U-boat commanders and their crewmembers in both world wars became public heroes at home and public enemies to the Allies.

THE GREATEST ACE

Lothar von Arnauld de la Perière commanded two U-boats during World War I. He sank more Allied ships than any other submariner of the war. He was so successful that his commanders assigned a cameraman to his crew to film his adventures.

BRAVE AND BOLD

Captain Günther Prien *(left)* receives congratulations from his commander, Grand Admiral Raeder. In 1939 Prien had sailed his U-boat into a heavily guarded British harbor and had sunk a battleship. His daring attack earned him the **Knight's Cross.** It also made him the most famous U-boat commander of World War II. Prien was lost at sea in 1941.

American Heroes

O'KANE

Commander Richard H. O'Kane commanded the USS *Tang*. It was one of the most successful submarines of the U.S. Pacific Fleet in World War II. O'Kane received the **Congressional Medal of Honor** in 1947. He retired from the navy in 1957.

USS *TANG*

On the night of October 25, 1944, the *Tang* single-handedly attacked a large convoy of Japanese ships. It caused major damage. But a faulty torpedo fired by the *Tang* reversed, sinking the American submarine. Only nine of the crew, including the ship's commander, survived.

>> **Congressional Medal of Honor** – the highest U.S. medal for bravery

The Silent Service

Submariners are unseen and unheard beneath the sea. They are sometimes called the Silent Service. During the world wars, submarine crews had to turn off their engines and avoid moving around the ship. Enemy warships equipped with **hydrophones** could hear such movement. By World War II, allied warships were equipped with the allied submarine detection investigation committee **(ASDIC)** equipment. ASDIC was much more efficient than the earlier hydrophones.

UNHEARD UNDERWATER

This German poster from World War I shows an anxious crew on board a U-boat. They are listening to the sound of an enemy warship above.

TRAGEDY

The USS *Thresher* was one of the U.S. Navy's first nuclear-powered attack submarines. In April 1963, the *Thresher* took part in a deep-sea diving exercise in the Atlantic Ocean. After reaching test depth, the submarine sent an alarm message. After that, nothing more was heard. Eventually, remains from the submarine came to the surface. The navy officially declared the *Thresher* lost. All 139 crewmembers died.

ONLY ONE

"The Captain tends to be a one-man band...because he is the only one who can see the target."

Commodore M. D. MacPhearson, Royal Navy submarine commander, World War II

Submarine Weapons

Submarine weapons are mostly attack weapons. They include torpedoes, missiles, and mines. They are designed to attack targets on land or at sea.

TORPEDOES

Since World War I, torpedoes have been the main strike weapons carried in submarines. Torpedoes are like miniature submarines. They contain explosive materials at the front. A guidance system is in the middle. A small electric motor in back drives the torpedo through the water.

UNSEEN UNDERWATER

Torpedoes are especially effective because they strike a ship below the waterline. Water rushes inside. This causes the boat to sink rapidly.

Missiles

Missiles are becoming the most widespread weapons used by submarines. Missiles can be launched from a submarine even while it is underwater. They can be used against surface ships or against targets on land.

TRIDENT

During tests in the Atlantic, a U.S. Navy nuclear-powered ballistic missile submarine launches a Trident C-4 missile. Trident can carry several warheads at once. It has a range of up to 4,000 miles.

POSEIDON

A Poseidon C-3 ballistic missile is launched from the nuclear-powered strategic missile submarine USS *Lafayette*. Poseidon was the main deterrent for the North Atlantic Treaty Organization (NATO) for more than forty years.

NUCLEAR REDUCTION

Held from 1969 to 1979, the Strategic Arms Limitation Talks (SALT) reduced the number of nuclear weapons in the world. Because of SALT, the U.S. Navy has converted some of its ballistic missile submarines into regular attack submarines. Attack submarines are only equipped with tactical weapons for nonnuclear combat.

>> SALT = meetings between the United States and the Soviet Union

Submarine Weapons

SUBHARPOON

Subharpoon is a submarine-launched anti-ship missile. It has a range of eighty miles. The radar-guided Subharpoons fly close to the surface, making them harder to find.

TOMAHAWK

A Tomahawk submarine-launched cruise missile (SLCM) soars into the sky. It was launched from the nuclear-powered attack submarine USS *La Jolla*.

>> **passive sonar** – a listening tool that does not send out any signal

Submarines sometimes carry sea mines. Mines are bombs that float in the water. They are set off by water pressure, by contact with enemy ships, or by submarines passing close by.

Sensors

Submarines rely on sensors when they are underwater. Sensors are devices that sense, or find, the presence of an enemy. Submarines use them as defense against attack or to locate an enemy.

SONAR BULGE

The bulge on the bow of this Canadian Oberon class submarine contains sound navigation and ranging (sonar) equipment. Many naval craft use sonar. It works like radar but uses sound waves rather than radio waves. **Passive sonar** listens for sounds, such as a motor. **Active sonar** transmits a sound wave. If the wave hits something in the water, an echo is sent back.

active sonar – a listening tool that bounces a signal off an enemy ship

Submarines in Action

Submarines have played a major part in the conflicts of the 1900s. Their operations helped end the wars. Submarines will continue to be an important part of modern warfare for years to come.

World War I

SINKING THE *LUSITANIA*

The RSM *Lusitania* was a British passenger ship. During the early years of World War I, it sailed regularly between Britain and the United States. Britain was at war with Germany, but the United States was not. The *Lusitania* left New York for Britain on May 1, 1915. While the ship was at sea, Germany declared **total war** on all shipping. It claimed that passenger ships were being used to carry weapons across the Atlantic. Near the Irish coast, a torpedo from submarine U-20 struck the *Lusitania*. The ship sank in 18 minutes. A total of 1,195 people died. Among them were 123 Americans. Public anger in the United States helped bring the nation into the war.

DREADFUL SIGHT

"It was the most dreadful sight of my life....I couldn't bring myself to launch the second torpedo among the struggling passengers, who deserved to succeed in saving themselves."

Captain Walther Schwieger,
Commander U-20, World War I

ENGINE ROOM

Inside the **engine room** of an oil-burning World War I U-boat. These early submarines were very uncomfortable. They were cold and damp and had very cramped living and working spaces.

>> **engine room** – the compartment of a ship containing the motor

Submarines in Action

In the early stages of World War II, submarine warfare mainly took place on the Atlantic and Mediterranean convoy routes. After 1941, however, important sea battles were also fought in the Pacific.

World War II

X-CRAFT AND *TIRPITZ*

In September 1943, six British X-Craft midget submarines (small submarines carrying just six people) crossed from Scotland to German-occupied Norway. Their target was Germany's huge 41,000-ton battleship, the *Tirpitz*. The *Tirpitz* was a major threat to Atlantic supply routes. Fear of the *Tirpitz* prevented Britain's Royal Navy from sending more warships to the Pacific. The X-Craft raiders caused enough damage to keep the *Tirpitz* out of the war for a year.

DAVID AND GOLIATH

One of the tiny X-Craft that crippled the mighty battleship *Tirpitz*

ATLANTIC U-BOAT SUNK

Crewmembers aboard the U.S. Coast Guard cutter *Spencer* watch their **depth charge** explode in the water, crippling the U-175. By 1943 Allied naval commanders knew from secret reports where enemy U-boats were being sent.

PACIFIC DESTROYER DESTROYED

A torpedoed Japanese destroyer is seen through the **periscope** of the submarine USS *Wahoo* in June 1943. Destroyers escorted cargo ships that were needed for Japan's war economy. The *Wahoo* and its crew were lost later in the year.

Submarines in Action

After World War II, nuclear-powered and nuclear-armed submarines appeared. They were used more for deterrence than for actual combat. Attack submarines remained important. They continue to operate as part of a modern naval fleet with nonnuclear weapons.

BELGRANO

The Argentine cruiser *Belgrano* sinks *(above)* during the 1982 Falklands War between Britain and Argentina. Crewmembers fly the Jolly Roger pirate flag after the British nuclear-powered attack submarine **HMS** *Conqueror (left)* sank the cruiser with two torpedoes on May 2. More than 360 lives were lost. The Argentine navy stayed in port for the rest of the conflict.

DESERT STORM

The USS *Louisville* returns to San Diego in April 1991. The *Louisville* was the first submarine to launch a land attack Tomahawk cruise missile in combat. Cruise missiles were used against Iraq after its invasion of neighboring Kuwait in 1990.

ENDURING FREEDOM

During **Operation Enduring Freedom** in 2002, crewmembers aboard the USS *Norfolk* inspect a Tomahawk cruise missile. They are about to load it into its launcher. Many SLCMs were launched against terrorist targets in Afghanistan. They helped to pave the way for international troops to move in.

>> **Operation Enduring Freedom** – a war against terrorists in Afghanistan

Life Aboard

Submarine life is very different from life on a surface vessel. It takes special qualities to live and work in a sealed tube deep below the surface of the ocean. The selection process and training for a submarine crew is more demanding than for most other armed forces.

Then and Now

U-BOAT LIFE

German submariners play cards in the cramped crew quarters aboard a World War II U-boat. They had to endure long patrols in enemy waters. They were constantly at risk from surface or air attack. There was no room for luxuries on board.

>> **tower** – the raised structure above the deck of a submarine

RUN SILENT, RUN DEEP

Crewmembers prepare to seal off the **tower** aboard a U.S. submarine during World War II. World War II submarines used battery-run electric motors to operate underwater. The **main engine** recharged the batteries while the ship was sailing on the surface. Electric motors were almost silent.

TRUE FOR ALL

"Submariners are a special brotherhood, either all come to the surface or no-one does. On a submarine, the phrase 'all for one and one for all' is not just a slogan, but reality."

Vice-Admiral Rudolf Golosov,
Russian Navy

WATCH AT WORK

Crewmembers aboard the USS *Seawolf* put this new fast attack submarine through sea trials in 2002.

Submarine Life

A U.S. Navy fast attack submarine carries a **complement** of 120 to 130. This crew is divided into departments, according to the jobs the crewmembers do. The Executive Department is in overall command. Navigation and Operations is in charge of the submarine's location and its communications. The Engineering Department takes care of the ship's engines and mechanical workings. The Combat Systems Department is in charge of the weapons carried on board.

NAVIGATION AND OPERATIONS

Submarine crewmembers practice navigation skills on a high-tech U.S. Navy simulator. The computerized device fakes real submarine movements.

EXECUTIVE DEPARTMENT

The commanding officer and chief navigation officer on the **sail** of the fast attack submarine USS *City of Corpus Christi*. They are guiding the ship out into the Caribbean Sea.

ENGINEERING

Engineers onboard an Upholder class Royal Canadian Navy submarine check its diesel-electric engine system. Diesel-electric engines are cheaper and easier to build than nuclear engines, although they are not as efficient.

COMBAT SYSTEMS

A weapons specialist aboard the nuclear-powered hunter-killer submarine USS *Seawolf*. He is checking the missile launch console.

Submarine Life

A large ballistic submarine is about 550 feet long and 40 feet wide. Yet most of the space is taken up with the equipment needed to control the ship and its weapons. The crew has to fit in wherever it can. Sometimes, crew bunks are in the same area where the torpedoes are stored.

USS *SEAWOLF*

A Seawolf class submarine is specially designed to attack enemy ballistic missile submarines. The *Seawolf* carries a crew of 130 officers and **enlisted**. It is the fastest tactical submarine in the U.S. Navy.

SEAWOLF WATCH

Crewmembers at the **watch** on the USS *Seawolf*

>> **enlisted** = crewmembers other than officers

An officer looks through the periscope of the attack submarine USS *Norfolk*. He is checking that the ocean is clear of enemy ships before allowing the sub to rise to the surface. Nuclear submarine crews sometimes stay underwater for several months.

HOUSE ROOM

"When your living space is basically the size of a three-bedroom house, and you've got about 120 people crammed in there, you develop a certain amount of consideration and civility, or you just don't survive."

Lieutenant Commander Dave Henry, U.S. Naval Reserve

Submarine Enemies

Submarines are among the most feared weapons of war. They can move unseen and strike by surprise. For this reason, submarines also face many enemies. Aircraft, warships, and missiles have been specially developed to find and destroy them.

CAT AND MOUSE

A German U-boat photographed from an attacking **B25** during World War II. Submarines in World War II had to spend long periods on the surface. Their battery-powered motors only lasted a few hours. Both sides used anti-submarine warfare (ASW) airplanes to hunt and sink surfaced enemy submarines.

HOVERING THREAT

A Sea Hawk SH60 ASW helicopter sits on the deck of the destroyer USS *Cushing*. The helicopter is probably the most effective weapon against submarines. Most ASW warships carry helicopters for tracking and attacking submarines. A helicopter can travel at similar speeds to a submarine and follow it. Because helicopters fly just above the ocean, they cannot be found by sonar or be attacked by torpedoes.

PENGUIN POWER

A U.S. Navy Sea Hawk ASW helicopter fires its **Penguin** anti-ship missile. The missile is effective against surfaced submarines. Traveling faster than the speed of sound, Penguin has its own radar guidance system.

Submarine Enemies

Some anti-submarine weapons have nuclear warheads, such as nuclear depth charges. Nuclear weapons are not precise. But they will destroy anything in the water for many miles around. Most conventional (nonnuclear) anti-submarine weapons rely on accurate target finding.

EYE IN THE SKY

A U.S. Navy P3 Orion ASW reconnaissance, or information-gathering, aircraft over the Pacific. The Orion is a long-range patrol aircraft. It provides accurate submarine tracking information to surface ships or strike aircraft.

WATCHFUL

A U.S. Navy anti-submarine warfare technician onboard a Navy Orion airplane. Her screen shows up ships on or under the ocean surface over a wide area, even through cloud or mist.

A U.S. Navy destroyer pursuing its target at high speed. Many warships have specific anti-submarine tasks. They are fitted with underwater **acoustic** and **electromagnetic sensors**. They also carry anti-submarine missiles, depth charges, and torpedoes.

SIGNATURE IN SOUND

"Each submarine has its own acoustic characteristics... when you hear Frank Sinatra over the radio, you don't have to be told it's Frank Sinatra, but you know who it is."

Rear Admiral Thomas W. Evans, U.S. Navy submarine commander, Cold War era (1945–1991)

Submarines

Like other warships, submarines are divided into classes. The United States has by far the world's largest submarine fleet. Other countries with significant numbers of submarines include Russia, China, Britain, and France.

USS *LOUISIANA*

The *Louisiana* is the last of the U.S. Navy's Ohio class ballistic missile submarines. These submarines provide the nation's primary nuclear deterrent. They can launch their missiles from any ocean to any continent on earth.

Details:
Crew: 15 officers, 140 enlisted
Length: 560 ft.
Beam: 42 ft.
Propulsion: 1 x nuclear reactor, 2 x steam turbines, 80,000 hp total, 1 shaft
Max Speed: 25 kts.
Displacement: 18,750 tons submerged
Armament: 24 missile tubes, 4 torpedo tubes

displacement—the volume of water moved aside by a floating object

HMS *VANGUARD*

The Vanguard class of nuclear-powered ballistic missile submarines is Britain's primary nuclear deterrent force. Vanguard class submarines are equipped with Trident missiles.

Details:
Crew: 143 total
Length: 490 ft.
Beam: 42 ft.
Propulsion: 1 x nuclear reactor, 1 x 27,500 steam turbine, 1 shaft
Max Speed: 25 kts.
Displacement: 15,865 tons submerged
Armament: 16 Trident missiles, 4 torpedo tubes

USS *TOLEDO*

The USS *Toledo* is a Los Angeles class nuclear-powered fast attack submarine. The class was designed specifically for **carrier battle group** escort tasks. They carry both torpedoes and Tomahawk cruise missiles.

Details:
Crew: 13 officers, 116 enlisted
Length: 360 ft.
Beam: 33 ft.
Propulsion: 1 x nuclear reactor, 35,000 hp, 1 shaft
Max Speed: 30 kts.
Displacement: 6,927 tons submerged
Armament: Tomahawk land attack missiles, 4 torpedo tubes

Submarines

Submarines range in size from the huge 550-foot long ballistic missile **"boomers"** to small research or rescue craft of about 50 feet. Nuclear-powered submarines are generally referred to as either **SSNs** or **SSBNs.**

USS *CONNECTICUT*

The *Connecticut* is the second of the two Seawolf class fast attack submarines in service with the U.S. Navy. Like the USS *Seawolf*, the *Connecticut* is much quieter than other fast attack submarines. Seawolf submarines are also the fastest in the U.S. Navy Fleet.

Details:
Crew: 12 officers, 121 enlisted
Length: 353 ft.
Beam: 40 ft.
Propulsion: 1 x nuclear reactor, 52,000 hp, 1 shaft
Max Speed: 35 kts.
Displacement: 9,137 tons submerged
Armament: 8 torpedo tubes

HMS *ASTUTE*

The *Astute* is an Astute class nuclear-powered hunter-killer submarine in service with Britain's Royal Navy. This new class will replace Britain's Swiftsure class attack submarines.

Details:
Crew: 109 total officers and crew
Length: 300 ft.
Beam: 32 ft. 6 in.
Propulsion: 1 x nuclear reactor, 1 x 15,000 steam turbine, 1 shaft
Max Speed: 30 kts. submerged
Displacement: 7,200 tons
Armament: 5 torpedo tubes

NR-1

The *NR-1* is a nuclear-powered research submarine built in the United States. It does deep-sea engineering and recovery work. The *NR-1* was used to find parts of the *Challenger* space shuttle lost in 1986.

Details:
Crew: 2 officers, 3 enlisted
Length: 150 ft.
Beam: 12 ft.
Propulsion: 1 x nuclear reactors, 2 x external motors, 2 shafts
Max Speed: 12 kts.
Displacement: 400 tons
Armament: none

Submarines

After World War II, the world's leading powers focused on developing ballistic missile submarines as a deterrent. Since the early 1990s, attention has turned toward building or adapting submarines to respond quickly to changing world situations.

USS *KEY WEST*

The USS *Key West* is a Los Angeles class nuclear-powered attack submarine. Los Angeles class submarines make up the bulk of the U.S. Navy's underwater strike force. The USS *Key West* is based at Pearl Harbor in the Philippines.

Details:
Crew: 14 officers, 126 enlisted
Length: 425 ft
Beam: 33 ft
Propulsion: 1 x nuclear reactor, 1 shaft
Max Speed: 21 kts
Displacement: 8,251 tons
Armament: 16 missile tubes

Le *Triomphant* is a French nuclear-powered ballistic missile submarine. The Triomphant class will consist of four submarines, replacing the earlier L'Inflexible class of ballistic missile submarines.

Details:
Crew: 15 officers, 96 enlisted
Length: 453 ft.
Beam: 41 ft.
Propulsion: 1 x nuclear reactor, 41,500 hp
  total, 1 shaft
Max Speed: 25 kts.
Displacement: 14,335 tons submerged
Armament: 18 missiles and torpedoes

MYSTIC

The *Mystic* rides on the back of the USS *La Jolla*. The *Avalon* and the *Mystic* are the U.S. Navy's two deep **submergence** rescue vehicles (DSRVs). They were developed after the USS Thresher accident in 1963. They are carried to the scene of an accident on the back of a larger submarine. They can reach depths of 5,000 feet below the surface.

Details:
Crew: 2 operators
Length: 50 ft.
Beam: 8 ft. diameter
Propulsion: 1 x electric motor, 1 shaft, 4 x **ducted thrusters**
Max Speed: n/a
Displacement: 36 tons
Capacity: 24 passengers

Future Submarines

Future submarines will be quieter and harder to find. They will be **multi-mission** ships. This means they will be able to switch from strategic deterrence to tactical strike roles as needed.

VIRGINIA CLASS

The Virginia is the new attack submarine (NAS) class of fast attack submarines. It will provide the U.S. Navy's main submarine strike force after the Los Angeles class ships are retired. Virginia class submarines will be equipped with land attack missiles, torpedoes, and mines.

NEW ATTACK SUBMARINE

This illustration of the inside of a NAS shows where the submarine's missiles are kept behind the sail. A small submersible is carried on top.

SPECIAL DELIVERIES

Some versions of the Virginia class NAS will have a new sail designed to fit future weapon systems. They will also be able to launch unmanned underwater vehicles and **SEAL** Special Forces delivery vehicles.

Future Submarines

Keeping its 150 or so crewmembers alive and well is one of the hardest jobs a submarine has to perform. Heat, light, food, air for breathing, and **accommodation** take up much of the equipment and space onboard. Naval planners in many countries are working on unmanned underwater vehicles (UUVs) as a less costly means of defense. UUVs also have the advantage that no lives are at risk.

Warfare without Warriors

DEEP-SEA DIVER

This U.S. Navy UUV can do many jobs that would be dangerous for a crewed submarine. Its tasks include finding enemy mines and working below the North Pole **icecap.**

>> **accommodation** – the living space required by crewmembers

Miniature Submarine Warfare

Miniature submarines with a single crewmember will become more effective in future undersea warfare. Small and silent, they will be hard to find. They will also be much easier to move than a large submarine.

DEEP-SEA FLYER

These illustrations show a new single-crew submersible concept called Deep Flight. It will be able to move like an underwater airplane. Craft such as Deep Flight will be able to operate from larger submarines, which will be used as bases. As well as scientific research, these submersibles could undertake military missions, including sabotage, reconnaissance, mine detecting, and rescue.

Hardware at a Glance

AA = anti-aircraft
ASROC = anti-submarine rocket
ASW = anti-submarine warfare
FAS = Future Attack Submarine
HMS = Her/His Majesty's Ship
NAS = New Attack Submarine
NATO = North Atlantic Treaty Organization
SALT = Strategic Arms Limitation Treaty
SLCM = submarine-launched cruise missile

SONAR = sound navigation and ranging
SSBN = strategic submarine ballistic nuclear
SSN = strategic submarine nuclear
SUBROC = submarine-launched rocket
UAV = unmanned aerial vehicle
U-boat = German submarine
USS = United States ship
UUV = unmanned undersea vehicle

Further Reading & Websites

Antram, Dave. *Ships and Submarines.* London: Franklin Watts Inc, 2000.

Bartlett, Richard. *United States Navy.* New York: Heinemann Library, 2003.

Chant, Christopher. *The History of the World's Warships.* New York: Book Sales, 2000.

Faulkner, Keith. *Jane's Warship Recognition Guide.* New York: HarperResource, 1999.

Gaines, Ann Graham. *The Navy in Action.* Berkeley Heights, NJ: Enslow Publishing, 2001.

Genat, R. *Modern U.S. Navy Submarines.* Osceola, WI: Motorbooks International, 1997.

Higgins, Christopher. *Nuclear Submarine Disasters.* Broomhall, PA: Chelsea House, 2001.

Humble, Richard. *Submarines & Ships.* New York: Viking Childrens Books, 2001.

Humble, Richard. *A World War II Submarine.* New York: Peter Bedrick Books, 2001.

Payan, Gregory. *Fast-Attack Submarine: The Seawolf Class.* Chicago: Children's Press, 2000.

Payan, Gregory. *Life on a Submarine.* Chicago: Children's Press, 2000.

Preston, Anthony. *Submarine Warfare: An Illustrated History.* San Diego, CA: Thunder Bay Press, 1999.

How submarines work <http://www.howstuffworks.com/submarine.htm>

Mk48 torpedo demo <http://www.navy.gov.au/fegs/submarines/mk48.html>

Submarine History <http://www.submarine-history.com>

U.S. Marine Corps <http://www.usmc.mil>

U.S. Navy <http://www.navy.mil>

U.S.S. Bowfin submarine museum <http://www.bowfin.org>

U.S.S. Ling submarine virtual tour <http://www.njnm.com>

Places to Visit

You can see examples of some of the submarines and related hardware contained in this book by visiting the naval and maritime museums listed here.

Arizona Memorial, Pearl Harbor, Honolulu, Hawaii <www.nps.gov/usar/>
Baltimore Maritime Museum, Baltimore, Maryland <www.baltomaritimemuseum.org>
Canadian War Museum. Ottawa, Ontario, Canada <www.civilization.ca/cwm/cwme.asp>
Great Lakes Naval Memorial & Museum, Muskegon, Michigan <www.silversides.org>
Hampton Roads Naval Museum, Norfolk, Virginia <www.hrnm.navy.mil>
Independence Seaport Museum, Philadelphia, Pennsylvania <http://seaport.philly.com>
Intrepid Sea-Air-Space Museum, New York, New York <www.intrepidmuseum.org>
Louisiana Naval War Memorial, Baton Rouge, Louisiana <www.usskidd.com>
Maritime Command Museum, Halifax, Nova Scotia, Canada
    <www.pspmembers.com/marcommuseum/>
National Museum of Naval Aviation, Pensacola, Florida <www.naval-air.org>
Naval Undersea Museum, Keyport, Washington <http://num.kpt.nuwc.navy.mil>
New Jersey Naval Museum, Hackensack, New Jersey <www.njnm.com>
Pacific Fleet Submarine Memorial Association, Honolulu, Hawaii
St. Mary's Submarine Museum, St Mary's, Georgia <http://stmaryssubmuseum.com>
San Diego Maritime Museum, San Diego, California <www.sdmaritime.com>
Submarine Force Museum, Groton, Connecticut <www.ussnautilus.org/museum.htm>
U.S. Naval Academy Museum, Annapolis, Maryland <www.usna.edu/museum>
Virginia War Museum, Newport News, Virginia <www.warmuseum.org>
Washington Navy Yard Museum, Washington, D.C.
    <www.history.navy.mil/branches/nhcorg8.htm>

Index

Picture Sources

BAe; 29 (t), 37 (t), 39 (t)
Defense Visual Information Center; 6, 7 (b), 9 (b), 17 (r), 18 (t), 21, 23, 25 (t), 32, 34 (t)
M K Dartford; 7 (t), 9 (t), 11 (b), 14, 17 (l), 26
France Navy; 41 (t)
John Batchelor; 31-32
Robert Hunt Library; 12, 20, 22, 24,

U.S. Navy; 8, 10, 11 (t), 13, 15, 16, 18 (b), 19, 25 (b), 27, 28, 29 (b), 31, 33, 34 (b), 35, 36, 37 (b), 38, 39, 40, 41 (b), 42, 43, 45